THERE IS NONE RIGHTEOUS

JIM REYNOLDS

WESTBOW
PRESS®
A DIVISION OF THOMAS NELSON
& ZONDERVAN

WestBow Press books may be ordered through booksellers or by contacting:

WestBow Press
A Division of Thomas Nelson & Zondervan
1663 Liberty Drive
Bloomington, IN 47403
www.westbowpress.com
844-714-3454

Scripture taken from the King James Version of the Bible.

ISBN: 978-1-6642-6909-5 (sc)
ISBN: 978-1-6642-6908-8 (e)

Library of Congress Control Number: 2022911180

Print information available on the last page.

WestBow Press rev. date: 06/15/2022

There is none that doeth good, no, not one... for that all have sinned:

Romans 3:12; 5:12

Introduction

Not long ago a father and mother called their two children, ages twelve and ten, in for a serious talk: "Your mother and I have decided it is time to talk to the two of you about your lack of worldly insight." He paused to see if the boy and girl were paying the required attention needed for this discussion: He then continued, "We've noticed for a long time now that neither of you have ever lied to us; nor stolen anything; and we suspect you have never cheated anyone. Most of all, we have noticed you haven't rebelled or even ever been angry towards us or anyone else."

The father most seriously continued: "Therefore, your mother and I have decided tomorrow she will take you to the library to get some books that will teach you how to lie; how to steal, cheat and most of all how to rebel: or at least how to get angry."

The next day at the library with the two children at her side, she asked the librarian where she could find books on how to teach children to lie, steal, cheat and become angry. "Oh, those would be on the self-help aisle", answered the librarian satisfactorily. However, the mother could not find any books that would help in teaching the children to lie, steal, cheat or rebel.

Now, that was a silly story, because we all know we are born with lying, stealing, cheating even rebellion in our souls. These things are natural. In fact, we have to teach our children not to lie, steal, cheat and control their tempers. Nevertheless, some of us learn to control these behaviors and we thus become labeled the "good" people despite still possessing this corrupt nature. We just don't show it, and by not showing it we conclude these flaws have in themselves disappeared.

This little book explores the humble and the humbled, and is based on actual facts taking place in a true setting in the mid seventies. Nevertheless, names of persons and places have been changed for obvious reasons.

As Christians, we are not to forget those in prison as if they are somehow different from those of us on the outside. Yes, they have committed a crime and must receive due punishment, however, their nature is that of our own: *"… There is none righteous, no, not one:(Romans 3:10).* All scripture quotes are from the *King James Version*.

Chapter One

The day was ordinary as they all were: Early, I pull up to the little minimum security Camp#73 nestled in the Blue Ridge Mountains on the outskirts of town. As usual, I walk to the guardhouse; say my "Hi" to the sergeant; make my stop in the restroom so I can be sure to make the whole day without a break. Of course, there is the normal Playboy centerfold tapped to the mirror. Leaving the restroom, the two guards and sergeant giggle because they are sure how that centerfold bothered me, but little did they know I was over such things; nevertheless, I silently let them have their fun. Finally, I walk across the compound between the dormitory and cafeteria up the three steps to the doublewide classroom where I was the teacher.

Soon the students would be making their way to the classroom. There would be anywhere from six to ten students depending on their mood. For each day of attendance the inmate would receive two hours compensation time towards early release. "Who cares", is the shrugged response to these behavior modification carrots.

William Red Cloud was always the first. He already had his high school degree, but would spend his whole day in the classroom at one of the typewriters. I had no idea what he wrote: never asked. Of course, often he would turn around and freely enter into any group interchanges. One thing about William: it was easily seen that he was bright and insightful. Also, he never bothered anyone and no one bothered him. He was in for murder: twenty years worth. "Hey William", as I acknowledge his presence.

He replies, "Hi Teach", as he takes his seat: He never signed the roll nor did I ask him to. Then come Ronald, Don and Ted, always in that order: each hoping to get their GED (Means: General Educational Development and is a certificate of high school equivalency). These three were a pleasure to have in attendance, but oh how far they would have to go to sit for the GED exam. Lots of work and more work is their future, but if hard work gets you a GED these three just might make it.

An hour or so later comes Fred. He needs his GED but knows he will never get it. By looking at him you would never know he had a severe learning disability. However, rather than expose this deficiency by trying he simply puts his day in the class getting his meager "comp" time and a sense of accomplishment by association. At times, someone asks a question out of context and I am not averse to taking time to delve into the issue. It is here Fred participates. So his presence isn't all futile, plus this involvement gives Fred some positive interpersonal skill development which he desperately needs.

Then the Old Man would make his way: find an empty table; take out his wallet, and place the picture of his daughter in front of him and not once say one word to anyone all day; then leave when class was over. From the start, I sensed a ritual here and left it as such. Later I would be told the "what for" and I am glad my instincts were correct: It seems some county officials of a neighboring very rural county wanted some out of state busybody eliminated. They made a deal with the Old Man: You do the dirty work and we will take care of your daughter for life and make sure you don't get the death penalty. Being destitute with no future, the Old Man obliged and the sheriff indeed took the most care for his daughter: Caring for her as his own. She graduated from a local college; became a teacher and married into a wonderful family. Yes, the Old Man was a legend there in those mountains: not a good thing, but legend nevertheless. Yet, sometimes I wonder who the good guys are. We can see the bad guys; that's easy, but who are the good guys: that is, if there are any? Nevertheless, he was a "lifer", and like William never signed the roll, thus I never knew his name and never asked.

Billy and Wesley would come and go and stay just long enough to get their names on the roll. They could care less about a GED. They simply played the system.

I had to have the roll into the office when class ended at one o'clock. The more on the roll the better for that is what the higher-ups look for: not how many actually earned their GED: but only how many were in attendance. The government funding was based on numbers, not achievement. So, the unwritten rule was to get as many on the roll as possible. However, before the government funding ended eleven would get their GED. You see, once a couple of the guys did pass the exam, others would enlist in the program until the classroom was nearly full at times. No matter, the government not once sought the number of successes; only how many were on the roll. By year's end the attendance sheet was nearly full. Thus, the state was happy; the Captain was happy, and I didn't mind. I liked my job. I liked the men and they liked me. There was respect.

Chapter Two

The "Runner" dashed up to the classroom door: I at my desk while the few students were working on their assignments; William at his typewriter; Fred sitting in the back content; and the Old Man gazing at the picture of his daughter: Pushing open the door he said, "Hey Teach, Captain wants to see yah."

"OK, be there shortly", and off he went.

I wasn't concerned anyone would act out while I was gone because William wouldn't tolerate such. Nobody messed with William. He was short, but strong; very strong. More so, however, he was full-blooded Native American, and you simply didn't mess with William. He liked order, and you didn't cause problems around William: you just didn't. Yes, quiet and unassuming, yet don't disturb him: that would be disrespect.

Up the steps; past the outer office into the Captain's large office with an equally large desk came, "Come in Jim. Have a seat."

"Thanks", looking around there was Lester Kirby, the administrative officer with legs drawn up in one of the two large leather chairs (He was a short wiry guy and always had his legs tucked under him or in some such position. He most often wore black pants with a black casual shirt); and a smiling Captain Flannigan. You always found the Captain immaculately dressed with coat and tie, but most of all was his hair: lots of it perfectly groomed with several waves in that tan almost blond hair: His wife was a beautician.

"Jim, you ever play softball?"

"Sure did Captain. In fact, I was pretty good."

"Good, good: we thought so", He continued, "We're doing an experiment here. The city has a slow pitch softball league and we entered the camp." Not pausing to gain a response the Captain continued, "After all our major function here is to integrate inmates back into society, and we want to see if fielding a team in the league will be of any benefit": there was a slight pause, "We need a coach, and that is where you come in." Looking for a reaction from me he continued, "How about it, Jim: We can't pay you, but…"

Without hesitation I said, "Sure, no problem: I wouldn't want to be paid anyway. It will work better this way anyhow."

"Great, great: There is a required league meeting at the Recreation Center tonight at 7:30. We have already paid the entrance fee. See Betty Landers. She is expecting you and will explain everything to you: any questions?"

"Captain, we will need equipment, uniforms and time to practice…" He cut me short, "We have the equipment, uniforms such as they are, and you can practice out behind the cafeteria. William Red Cloud will show you where everything is", gesturing that the conversation was over. I made my way to the door when he called to me, "One thing I must insist upon: You must play Red Cloud every game, all game. Got that?"

You always faced the Captain when speaking to him, so turning I said, "Sure, no problem", as I thought to myself, "What a strange request." Nevertheless, I didn't give it another thought as I left the office.

Chapter Three

By the time I returned to the classroom I was already greeted with several, "Hi Coach", and William saying, "Come, I'll show you where all the equipment is." As I was finding out: nothing is private at a prison, and it sure does travel fast.

Sure enough, William unlocked the door to a shed next to the cafeteria and I was astonished to see bats, gloves and parts of ten uniforms (pants only, white with blue pinstripes; each player would have to supply his own white T-shirt and his own hat; that is if he wore one at all. Most wouldn't even wear a hat. However, one would wear a white headband and cut off sleeves; another, his Vietnam Army Bold Flat Top O.D. Hat; yet another would proudly wear a black and gold Wake Forest University ball cap: Yes, by all appearances you could call this a rag-tag team, but appearances can be deceiving as many would find out). Most of all, there were no cleats. Thinking to myself, "We must have cleats in these mountains; especially for the outfield grass". Then William commented, "Coach, we played a couple games against other camps, but never civilians. We weren't much good, but I know most of the guys, and we can practice later this afternoon: If that's OK?"

"Yeah, after class", I whispered more to myself than anyone else; thinking how I was going to put all this together.

That evening some twenty-six teams were represented and Betty was thrilled to announce, "The prison camp is entering a team this year guys. Jim here will be their coach." I knew only a few of the other coaches, but was familiar with the league itself. I had played on one of the teams some years ago and knew the process.

At the beginning of the season would be a tournament in which to seed the teams. Then there would be some fifteen scheduled games, and finally a tournament at the end of the season to determine a champion. We were scheduled to play tomorrow night against the Crusaders, last year's champs.

Lester Kirby thought that was great, just great.

"But Mr. Kirby, I don't even have a team. We haven't practiced, and no cleats for the outfielders. You can't play on grass here at night without cleats. That grass is like ice at night.

You know how it is."

"Jim, just do the best you can. William has been talking things up. He has scratched up a team already and is waiting out behind the cafeteria for practice." He continued, "We know you will do fine. We are counting on you": And with a slap on the back, I went to see my team.

Chapter Four

Fred had self appointed his self as our first baseman. It wouldn't take me long to find out why. Also, William was designated short outfielder by choice for the same reason as Fred: both were so muscle bound and neither one could throw the ball worth squat, and those two positions required the least amount of throwing. As it turned out, Fred would play only that first game. It seems he crossed Captain Flannigan and was shipped out to a maximum security prison two days later. You didn't cross the Captain. The Captain appears easy going, however he is anything but.

The rest of the team was just names and faces to me: mostly just faces. We went out back and I watched as some played catch; others attempted "pepper" for there wasn't enough room for any kind of batting practice: and all I could do was to observe a pending disaster.

Somehow I had to get the Captain's attention. He and Mr. Kirby were too flippant over this project, and no way did I want to be identified with this looming calamity. More so, these men didn't need to be humiliated as they were being set up to be by the system.

You see, the system says these guys are losers and the system is set out to prove it once again by placing these guys in an unwinnable situation only to prove the system to be right: these losers are losers and will always be losers. We try and help them, but they just won't be helped is the rational of the "good-guys".

While watching, I concluded: "I must find a way to get the Captain's attention." My three pigs obliged.

When I went home that afternoon to our log cabin, the pigs were out: all three of them heading for our neighbor's garden. Luckily, I had spare feed and lured them back to their space, but mending the fence would take much longer. So a quick convenient call to the Captain: "Sorry Captain, I won't make the game tonight. My pigs got out and it will take awhile to fix the fencing."

I didn't lie, but I knew and he knew it doesn't take four hours to fix a fence. He also knew exactly why I wasn't going to be at that first game. It worked. I had his attention.

We lost 56 to 6. Worse than that; it was a clown show and the packed stands were entertained to a bunch of losers losing as losers lose.

With no cleats the outfielders were sliding on their seats more than their feet chasing line drives after line drive. On our sideline and in the dugout arguments after argument prevailed, with bickering and finger pointing. This was pure laughing entertainment for hundreds watching. Even Logan, the guard, was embarrassed. After all, what can you expect from a bunch of convicts?

Next morning the "Runner" met me before I could reach the classroom, and without a word I knew Captain Flannigan wanted to see me.

Quit seriously he said, "OK Jim, what do you want?"

I quickly replied just as seriously: "We must have cleats for the outfielders and we must have at least two practices at a true ballpark. Our first game is next week."

Conceding he said, "You've got the cleats, but only one practice. That's all I can give you." He added, "Get with Kirby here to schedule the practice...and Jim, don't you miss anymore games."

"I won't Captain. Those pigs won't get out again", as I smiled.

He smiled... he liked cleaver men.

Chapter Five

The next four days were something else: I'd look up from my desk and here was Lieutenant Peterson with one of his recruits from Central Prison: "Here's your second baseman you need." Smiling, he presented Smith to me however we would all call him "Smitty". He was a doubtful looking specimen: small in stature; little on the old side, but he had a steely look in his eyes suggesting he knew what he was doing. I later found out he was indeed crafty, not only with the bat, but as sure a fielder as ever there was one: quick and sure, but lacked out and out speed due to being out of shape. Also, "Smitty" became an immediate "dorm boss" due to the notoriety of his crime and his intolerance towards any dissidence. He was one tough guy as well as being a decorated Vietnam veteran.

Next came Palmer my catcher to be: big, strong and fast. He looked more like a NFL halfback, and that is why:

he was a halfback: the top high school running back in the state some six years ago: but no grades...no grades. One thing for sure, nobody would run over this guy. He was fearless, yet the nicest guy you'd ever want to meet. One problem: he couldn't see without glasses, and he wouldn't wear glasses: "What would people think", he would reply. Yes, he could catch the slow arching pitch from the pitcher, but he could never see the ball being thrown in from an outfielder, especially at night games. I would have to make arrangements with whoever the pitcher was to field those throws much to Palmer's chagrin.

Lieutenant Peterson was having the time of his life: always a sports-nut, now he was a general manager of his very own team: Camp#73. He would find the recruit and Mr. Kirby would secure the inmates transfer. Not only did the Lieutenant know pro and college sports, he, over the years, knew every high school prospect and even others outside organized sports such as Bigfoot.

Now, one must take a deep breath when meeting Bigfoot: a true seven footer: not just tall, but strong and well built to go with that height, and he was exceptionally coordinated for such a stature. Where the Lieutenant found Bigfoot is the genius the Lieutenant possessed, and with each delivery for the team the Lieutenant grew prouder and prouder of himself. However, I would be confounded by what he came up with next.

Chapter Six

The following morning, as proud as a new papa, Lieutenant Peterson opened the door to the classroom announcing, "Here is your team captain and shortstop: meet Allen Kershaw, the best athlete to come out of this county... ever... Everybody calls him Al."

Dumbfounded, I looked with mouth wide open, thinking, "This is his prize recruit? Why it can't be, the guy is...well, outside his size, he sure doesn't look athletic...plus he had to be in his late thirties or early forties." However, before I could even say "hi", Lieutenant Peterson with arm around Allen's shoulders said, "Come on Al, I'll show you to your bunk": and off they went to the cafeteria bunk house.

You see, Al is a negotiator and that was the condition for playing on the camp's team: he would not bunk in the dormitory with eighty other guys. Plus, being a cook gave him four hours compensation time towards early release for every day served; not to mention being close to the food.

I would find out later Al was indeed an exceptional talent. Out of high school, Al had multiple full major college scholarship offers in both basketball and baseball. Instead, he joined the Navy. Al was to be the best athlete I would ever see in person, and how he moved that body from one place to another so effortlessly and quickly was enchanting to watch. Smooth could not define his movements, and his fielding and throwing were flawless. Being older, however, curbed his power in hitting. Nevertheless, he could place that ball wherever he wanted. The Lieutenant was correct: Al would become the captain and spokesman for the team. He was a natural leader and I surely needed him. Yes, how we all needed Al, our inspiration and leader.

Next came Red: What can be said about Red: He was fast, strong and an exceptional ballhawk. He never once made an error. No question, he was our centerfielder, and most of all he added youth to our otherwise slightly aged nucleus.

This ended Lieutenant Peterson's and Mr. Kirby's exploits leaving me to fill the rest of the team from what I could find in the dorm. This was going to be difficult after losing 56 to 6 in such a humiliating fashion, but I had help: Al.

Seeing me in thought, Al said, "I'll get what we need for Saturday's practice", as he headed for the dorm.

Chapter Seven

Mr. Kirby reserved one of the four practice fields across from the middle school for all Saturday afternoon before our first regular season game on the following Monday. It was here the team was formed.

Off and on during practice Al would stand with me discussing the in and out's of the team he had gathered from the dorm to complement those the Lieutenant had recruited.

First there was young Wilson. He was good, real good, but not as good as Al at shortstop, but Al was thinking what I was: "Jim (He would not call me "Coach". Al had authority issues), I'll move to third that way Wilson plays short stop. I can handle third base better than Wilson can and there isn't that much drop-off with Wilson at short."

"That's a plan", I replied.

Al and I continued: He knew the men and I concurred with each suggestion: Holder was fast and conspicuously cunning: he could be nowhere and everywhere at the same time. The opposing teams never knew where he would be next. Therefore, we would put him next to William Red Cloud in left field, because William was so slow (For some reason, I had always thought Native Americans were fast a foot, but not William. As hard as he tried, he remained excessively slow). Oh well, sense we had to play him every game, all game, we would squeeze him up as close to the left field foul line giving Holder most of left field to cover.

Since Red already was in centerfield, Pennington was to be the right fielder (You see, in slow pitch softball there are ten, rather than nine players, on each team with four of the ten in the outfield). Now Pennington was something else: six foot four; handsomely built with lightening speed and sure hands. Any or all NFL teams would cheat to draft him as a wide receiver: but he was slow on the thinking side of things.

This left Monroe as our pitcher: somewhat of a problem here: tall and skinny with huge horned rim glasses, and worse of all he insisted on batting cross-handed. Leaving Al's side, and going up to Monroe during his batting practice I said: "Monroe…Monroe, you can't hit the ball out of the infield cross-handed like that. You'll be a sure out each time up."

Not fazed and still in his crouched stance, he looked up at me: "Coach, I don't need to hit it out of the infield", and he went right back to dribbling ball after ball to the infield. It would have to do, because we didn't have anyone else to pitch. Besides, Monroe would prove to be a very effective pitcher with a gifted touch that would throw off unsuspecting batters. In addition, he was calm under fire. No amount of pressure could rattle him (I found out later Monroe was an undercover informant for the FBI. He wasn't there to inform on the other inmates. In fact, he was to inform on government officials in an adjoining county. Yes, he had been involved with a murder of a drug lord who had connections with those government officials; and of all things, he was here in this camp for protection from those big shots. The inmates here knew this and provided the needed protection. He could not have been in a safer place. No wonder pitching for a slow pitch softball team was "peanuts" for this guy). Fred was scheduled to be our first baseman, but by Monday he would be on his way to the maximum security prison. Thus, Bigfoot now had first base locked up. That is where I wanted Bigfoot anyway, and by Fred being transferred I didn't have to decide between the two men.

We now had ten men, but did we have a team? Yes, Camp#73 was to play its first regular season game in two days. We had the state prison system's finest athletes, but could they play as a team. This mountain league was good, real good: we had to be better. After all, slow pitch softball was the passion in these parts; seeing there were no major colleges or professional sports teams within hundreds of miles. Plus, we must remember TV was nearly nonexistent in these remote mountain communities in the mid seventies. Not until satellites did these places finally get any decent reception. Until then slow pitch softball consumed these folk.

Monday we would find out how good we really were.

Chapter Eight

We lost. It wasn't so much that we lost to the lowest seeded team (which meant we were the second lowest seed), but it was how we lost. With the talent of an elite team we looked awful. I should have guessed it when the camp bus pulled up to the ball park that Monday afternoon: each man exited the bus looking down and embarrassed to be there: That is, except Al who was the only one to look me in the eyes as I directed the players to our assigned dugout. You would have thought they were going to a funeral: then came, out of nowhere, this bright red pickup zooming into the parking lot. Several of the guys commented, "Here's the Chief." Yep, it was Chief Red Cloud, William's dad, and William's sisters piled in the back: The reservation was just down the other side of Rabbit Skin Pass near the prison. Now I knew why Captain Flannigan demanded I play William every minute of every game.

The Chief would be at every game just as the Captain figured he would (The only reason the Chief didn't make the first game was of the short notice: Just as well, the Chief would have been insulted at that 56 to 6 loss).

Like clockwork just before each game Chief Red Cloud would bring that pickup to a screeching dust covered halt, dismount that pickup in his typical red ball cap, red T-shirt and worn blue jeans; go to the top bench of the grandstands, fold his arms over his barrel chest; completely expressionless and never moving; and when the game was over remount that pickup; and off he and the girls would go until the next game (Where the girls went during the game was a mystery. However, without fail they were always ready and waiting in the truck when it was time to leave). I must say, Captain Flannigan was a wise man: a wise man indeed.

After the game I asked Al why the team played so poorly: "They were embarrassed for being laughed at that first game against the Crusaders."

"But that was then, this in now", I countered.

"Jim, you don't understand. We don't really want to be here. This isn't our thing: It's yours".

Oh my, he was right. Reality had just slapped me in the face. We were using these guys as pawns. Sure, who wouldn't want to be transferred from a maximum security prison to the softest camp in the state with the possibility of early release if only you go along with the program: But to expose oneself to ridicule…well, that wasn't part of the bargain.

Boy, oh boy how do I conjoin achieving a goal and at the same time preserving the dignity of men who don't think they have any dignity to preserve.

Chapter Nine

The next four games were much of the same: the guys simply going through the motions and content that the only fans to watch their games were William's father and sisters. All our games were afternoon because the evening games were for the top seeds and that's where the crowds were. So our low seed was a blessing in disguise: empty stands. That is until our fifth game against our first middle seeded team.

Logan pulled the camp bus up earlier than usual; even before Chief Red Cloud arrived. In the stands were six of the loveliest girls all in short shorts and very attractive. One asked, "Do you play the Warriors today?"

I replied, "No, that game was moved to the Dellwood field." Pausing as they took that in,

I continued, "Do you know where that is?"

They weren't paying the least attention to me. Their eyes were on ten gladiators making their way across the diamond to our dugout. Smiling they said in unison, "We'll just stay and watch your game." With that, ten heads snapped up in astonishment. Something changed: something big had just happened. The girls smiled at their new found warriors, and in unison the ten smiled back. Yes, at that moment we became a team: not ten gifted athletes. All of a sudden, there was a new reason to play: This was their game now, and no longer do they play for the system: each game now was personal: personal for each man individually and for the team collectively. They would now use the system; rather than the system using them: and of course, none of this change was thought out or calculate. It just happened; that's all.

From that moment, my coaching job became a breeze. The guys were awesome. The other team didn't stand a chance. We annihilated them, but it wasn't so much that we won and won big, but how we won: flawless defense, hitting and running with confidence, and heads held high, and then there was passion: passion for the game and for themselves.

During the game I noticed Pennington was going for a homerun and I cautioned him, "Hey Pennington, they are playing you too deep. Don't hit it long; go for a double in the gap" (There was no fence, just lots and lots of grass; so the outfielders could play all the way out to the light poles and beyond). However, he gave me a deadpanned look; shrugged his shoulders and said, "Watch this Coach", and for the girls' sakes, he hit the ball so hard he could have all but walked around the bases despite how deep the outfielders were playing him: and as Pennington was disposed to do, he did his skip-run technique around the bases. Now that sounds strange, but Pennington was so fast and big he had to skip to stay in the base paths. Running he couldn't turn the bases, thus the only way to make the turn on the base paths he developed this skip method. You'd have to see it to believe it.

Then there was Monroe: As usual, he would use that cross-handed batting grip, and as usual he dribbled the ball to the third baseman, but this time, with the girls watching, before the infielder even picked up the ball to throw to first, Monroe had long past reached first base. My jaw hung down. I had never seen anyone run so fast. Seeing my surprise, the others while laughing said, "Hey Coach, Monroe was state champ in the four forty in high school. Another laughed, "He still holds the state record."

Game after game I remained astonished at how good this team was, and so too was Betty Landers and the other league officials. They took notice as we eliminated our next four opponents handily.

A schedule change came out: our last five games were all to be night games. The pressure was on, nevertheless we were even more unstoppable, and the guys knew it. No longer did they come off the bus with heads down. No, no each man stepped down; looked me in the eyes; looked around as if to say, "We are unstoppable." Yes, we had become the main attraction in this mountain town. Crowds came to see these guys from Camp#73. No longer were they losers expected to lose, but a team to be reckoned with. Not to mention, we were the only team with any African Americans. We had five, with four whites and one Native American. That meant for even more buzz in the community. Also, many of the guy's families showed up for these night games (most, if not all of them worked and couldn't make the day games). Thus, the stands behind our dugout were packed out as well. The Chief wasn't alone any longer there on the top bleacher with arms folded; and if you looked carefully you could see a slight smile surfacing.

Then came the season ending tournament to crown the league champion, and our first tournament game would be with, of all teams, the top seeded police team called the Enforcers.

They were good, real good.

Chapter Ten

The "Runner", out of breath, pushed open the classroom door blurting, "Hey Teach, Captain wants to see you real fast!"

"OK, I'll be there soon", I replied from my desk facing the door.

"No, no Teach, he wants to see you now: like right now! I'm not to come back without you", as he waited impatiently for me to lead the way.

As the two of us were going up the few steps to the administration building, bursting out the door came three burley men in police uniforms nearly barreling over us; that is, if we hadn't stepped back. They were belly-laughing and slapping each other on their backs. They never saw us or acknowledged us as they headed for the squad car parked outside the gate. I knew exactly who they where: Who didn't know police Chief Earnhardt and his two sidekicks.

As I scooted past the office crew into the Captain's office, I was greeted with a most serious Captain Flannigan and a somber Lester Kirby. The tension in that room was thick: "Jim, you know who those guys are who just left?"

"Yes sir, police Chief Earnhardt and his deputies", I replied focusing in order to ascertain the meaning of all this urgency. The next words would explain it all.

"You play the police team tonight, right": His voice was very matter of fact.

"Yes sir, we are the main event tonight."

Still stone cold serious, he said, "You are going to win tonight." I didn't know if he was making a statement or asking a question as I replied, "We will do the best we can…" With his hand he stopped me short: he then paused for emphasis, "Jim, you will win. If not, don't come to work tomorrow. You won't have a job."

"Strange", I thought as I looked at him questioningly. He saw the confusion: "I mean it. If you lose tonight don't come to work tomorrow." Then slowly and deliberately he continued: "I don't want to ever see you here again if you lose."

It clicked. He was trying to tell me without having to say it out loud: There was big money riding on this game tonight. How much; I would never find out, but you know something; I wasn't worried at all. Somehow I knew at that moment we were going to win, and I gave him a quick smile; turned and left.

As I passed the office staff, they were all standing and watching me intently for any signs of doubt I might be projecting. Then on the way back to the classroom all eyes from the dorm, guardhouse and cafeteria were on me. Did I show any hesitation; any uncertainty; and then there was Al standing in the cafeteria doorway: Our eyes met and we were both thinking the same thing: "This night is ours!" We both nodded our approval. The whole camp saw this silent exchange, and they too knew: "This night is ours!" No longer were these ten men playing for themselves or for the team: they were now playing for the camp and for Captain Flannigan as well: After all, he had just bet that they were winners.

That evening, as the team went to the bus, the whole camp turned out forming two lines making a human tunnel from the dorm to the guard house. There was total silence as the ten gladiators walked confidently to the bus. Even the guards were standing.

By the time the bus arrived at the field; the place was packed to overflow. Fans were lining each sideline all the way to the light poles in the outfield; and as the bus pulled up to its' spot behind the stands most stood to watch our guys exit the bus: Never were the ten so sure. I was proud as I could be as each greeted me; looked at the crowd; nodded to the police team as if to say, "This night is ours!"

That is a lot to say, because the police team wasn't to be fooled with. They were as tough as they looked and then some. You would have thought they were Navy SEALS: each one chiseled to perfection in their full blue and silver uniforms, as opposed to our makeshift rag-tag uniforms. Besides their physical stature, they had been playing together for years and each of those years they were contenders for the championship. We would have to play the best game of our lives against the best team we would ever face (During the regular season they easily beat the Crusaders: you remember; the team that beat us 56 to 6).

We were assigned the first base dugout and were the home team, meaning we had the last at bats, which is always an advantage. We would need that.

Chapter Eleven

T hey scored first, but we responded to take the lead. Then for several innings both teams went scoreless. Finally, we went ahead by several runs, and they too responded to take the lead back.

Never had I seen such a tightly contested slow pitch game: usually in slow pitch both teams score double digit runs on a continuous basis: not so in this game. Here both teams were masterful.

About the fifth inning, I looked way out past the light poles into the dark to a little side road on a hill: a car was parked and someone in a white shirt and binoculars was watching the game from there: It had to be Captain Flannigan.

Slow pitch softball is a seven inning game. The team with the most runs at the end of seven innings wins. If there is a tie at the end of seven you go into extra innings until one team wins; however long that takes.

The Enforcers went ahead in the top of their seventh. I took a quick glance out to that guy in the white shirt and binoculars: he was gone. I guess Captain Flannigan couldn't stand it. Too bad, because we tied the game up in our bottom half of the seventh inning to throw the game into extra innings. Could we hold them scoreless? We had to; just had to, for I didn't know if we could out last them. They were in such better shape than our guys, and a long game is to their advantage. We had to stop them in their half of this inning, and then find a way to score just one run in our half of the eighth inning.

I noticed something with their leadoff batter in the top of the eighth inning: He was eyeing the right field line as he approached the batter's box. I'd seen this guy before: as a left hand hitter, at times, he would hit the ball on a line shot just inside the right field foul line making it impossible to stop, and with no fence; at night, on this grass it would be an easy home run. I knew what he was thinking: So, I waved Pennington in and over to the foul line. He looked at me; moved a few small steps my way, but not nearly enough. I waved to him again; and again he moved just a step or two. Finally, I yelled, "Time out ump", and I ran out to the spot I wanted Pennington to position himself. He continued to look at me with doubt. I then took my foot and carved a big X into the grass and said, "Right here: this is where I want you, right here", pointing to the X. "OK ump", and back to our dugout I went.

Sure enough, that guy hit the next pitch on a line shot right into the glove where Pennington was standing. He didn't have to move an inch. In fact, Pennington didn't have to move his glove: pop! (That shows you how arrogant that police team was: despite our plugging the hole that policeman was going for it anyway: advantage Camp#73). "See that Pennington, good job", I yelled at him. He yelled back, "Yeah Coach, but it's no fun your way." Nevertheless, that saved a sure home run, and the guys shut them down to close out their half of the inning and with that it was our turn to bat in the bottom of the eighth inning. This was "do or die" for us because the guys were getting tired. I don't know if we could last another inning. We had to win now: just had to.

All game long the catcher for the Enforcers trashed talked each of our players as they came to bat. He wasn't shy about it either. He went on and on with his verbal assault in an effort to distract us. It was his way to gain an edge. It wasn't working all that well, so as the game became tighter and tighter he increased his trash talking knowing none of our guys could respond in kind: being convicts and all. However, it was indeed getting to Al; seeing that he was the leader and spokesman for the team. Plus, Al had authority issues, and he naturally took insults more personally than the others. "Smitty" was also on edge, and the others watching Al weren't far behind: All this set Logan, the guard, into a nervous twitch.

I could see Al was at the boiling point, and the catcher also took notice: his strategy was working: At least it was working on Al. The tension from the game itself had increased with each inning, and the tension produced by the trash talking catcher signaled advantage Enforcers.

Somehow we had to score at this at bat before there was a riot lead by Al.

Chapter Twelve

I sensed this at bat was our last chance. We win this inning or one of two things happen; possibly both things happen: number one, we lose and that means Captain Flannigan loses. If he loses, we all lose and these guys are super losers again: "Can't count on a bunch of convicts." Oh, I wasn't worried about losing my job: I could always get another. These guys don't get another chance. Also, if we lose and the catcher says the wrong thing there is no telling what Al and the team would do. With only one lone unarmed guard, Logan, there would be no stopping a full scale combat of ten gladiators against ten trained and hardened policemen. No telling how far reaching this thing might go.

The fans were beginning to sense the tension as well. This game had turned into more than a competition between two passionate talented teams. It was fast becoming personal, and a silence was slowly engulfing the entire ballpark.

We had hit into two quick outs, and Al was up next. He had been having a bad day at the plate: always popping up to shallow centerfield. I knew what his problem was: his stride was uncharacteristically too long: all in an effort to hit the ball so hard as to silence that catcher. Thus, Al's back shoulder was dropping down causing the bat to have an upward swing; thus elevating the ball high in the air for an easy out. The added problem was: Al didn't take advice well. Nevertheless, I had to find a way to tell him. So, as he was squatted down in the on deck circle waiting for his turn to bat, I quietly squatted next to him and whispered, "You are striding too long. Cut your stride down by six inches and you won't pop up." Then I slipped back to the dugout.

It worked: with two outs Al drove the ball on a line shot for an easy stand up double. Up next came Bigfoot. If he could only get a clean hit Al could score and the game would be ours.

Bigfoot did better. He crushed the ball into the gap. Those outfielders never saw it zoom past them on the way to the next county. Al could walk home with the winning run. Instead, I looked up and saw Al running at full speed around third base and heading for home. More than that, Al had already lowered his shoulder as to take someone out. Then I saw what he was doing: The catcher for the Enforcers was innocently standing in the base path there at home plate looking to the outfield watching the fielders fetch Bigfoot's blast; conceding the winning run to us. Al had fire in his eyes as he headed full steam at the catcher. Al no longer cared about that winning run. He was going to take out that loudmouth. After all, the catcher was in the runner's way so Al, by all rights, could take him out according to the rules of the game: but why do it? It wasn't necessary: that didn't matter to Al. The fans also saw the impending collision. The place went silent, deathly silent.

I leaped out of the dugout; ran out towards home plate; held my hands up high as a stop sign to Al, and yelled as loud as I could, "NO AL, NO!"

With that, the police team stopped play to see what all the yelling was about amongst the total silence, and they saw this raging bull ready to take out their unsuspecting teammate as well as all our guys rising up out of the dugout ready to storm the field to protect their leader. Ten gladiators facing ten hardened policemen in front of hundreds of stunned fans: This was the making of a catastrophe.

I yelled again, "NO AL, NO!"

He pulled up inches short of the oblivious catcher; stepped around him; delicately tagged home plate, and on his way to the dugout he whispered to me, "thanks Coach."

There was no celebration on our part or for our fans: just relief: That is, except for Chief Red Cloud who was carrying a big smile. You know, I think he would have joined in on the brawl if it had taken place that night.

We gathered up our equipment as we always did and as we were walking to the bus, for some reason, we all stopped; turned, as one, to look out over the field for the last time: The entire police team was standing at attention in our honor. Our guys upon seeing this act of respect, again as one, nodded their approval in response. At least for the moment there was a bond between the humble and the humbled. Then the ten turned and entered the bus for Camp#73.

Chapter Thirteen

The day was ordinary as they all were. Early, I pull up to the little minimum security Camp#73 nestled in the Blue Ridge Mountains on the outskirts of town. As usual, I walk to the guardhouse; say my "Hi" to the sergeant; make my stop in the restroom so I can be sure to make the whole day without a break. However, this day there is no centerfold tapped to the mirror. Leaving the restroom, instead of giggling, the two guards and sergeant nod their respects to me. Finally, I walk across the compound between the dormitory and the cafeteria; up the three steps to the doublewide classroom where I was the teacher.

Soon the students would be making their way to the classroom. There would be anywhere from six to ten students depending on their mood… There would be no "Runner" today: no need: all was well at Camp#73.

And he put forth a parable to those which were bidden, when he marked how they chose out the chief rooms; saying unto them, When thou art bidden of any man to a wedding, sit not down in the highest room; lest a more honourable man than thou be bidden of him; and he that bade thee and him come and say to thee, Give this man place; and thou begin with shame to take the lowest room. But when thou art bidden, go and sit down in the lowest room; that when he that bade thee cometh, he may say unto thee, Friend go up higher: … For whosoever exalteth himself shall be abased; and he that humbleth himself shall be exalted. (Luke 14: 7-11)

Epilogue

We narrowly lost the next game making it our last game of the season. We played well, but there was nothing to prove anymore. Besides, the camp team won the "Best Sportsmanship" award. Interestingly, this trophy was bigger than the championship trophy awarded to last year's champs and again this year's champs, the Crusaders (I heard through the grapevine the Crusaders were thankful they didn't have to play us again after how we handled the Enforcers, and knowing we would seek revenge for the 56 to 6 shellacking they gave us that first game. They were also breathing a sigh of relief that we knocked off the Enforcers: No way did they want a rematch with the police team either).

Captain Flannigan would retire in a few months driving away in a brand new fancy car. Al would get early release and is doing well. That is except for the few days he had to spend in jail for urinating on Judge Ledbetter's lawn one night. Oh, Al wasn't drunk for he didn't drink, but he did have authority issues. Except for William Red Cloud, Monroe and not surprisingly "Smitty" all the others were granted early release due to Captain Flannigan's recommendations.

Me? My contract was for only one year and before we could sign another I was called to the minister in another state. Eventually Camp#73 would be shut down and converted to a community shelter including a kitchen program to feed and train residents.

Printed in the United States
by Baker & Taylor Publisher Services